Orchard Days

Poems from Dragon Orchard

Dedicated to Babs Stanier
who nurtured the orchard
and held it in her heart
1922 - 2007

Poems by Charles Bennett

Prose by Norman Stanier

Photographs by Richard Crompton

Inspiration by Ann Stanier

Index

Poetry Walk Map

Introduction

Our small corner of Herefordshire has long and distinguished connections with poetry. The links between the love of the land and the written word have been celebrated here by Elizabeth Barrett Browning, John Masefield and by The Dymock Poets including Rupert Brooke, Robert Frost, Wilfred Gibson and Edward Thomas.

Our family has been farming in Putley for many centuries and Great Grandfather Taylor planted up the Putley Court Estate with fruit trees for Squire Riley, who considered even John Masefield an unworthy suitor for his daughters. Our connections with the Ledbury Poetry Festival have led us to share cider with Andrew Motion and Carol Ann Duffy who have both enjoyed a glass of our aptly named Putley Gold.

The fruit of our twelve monthly meetings with Charles Bennett has given rise to these seasonal reflections. They bring together with grace and sensitivity the peace, pace and plenitude of our year.

Whether you visit us in person, through this book or via our website, we hope that you will smell the blossom, savour a ripe apple or juicy pear, sup our Cider and Juice and be beguiled by the sharp outline of a branch against a stark winter sky.

Our Orchard and Way of Life have been gently enhanced by Charles' inspirational and thoughtful work. Look or read, sit or stroll, wander or simply muse as you join us on this bucolic journey through our year.

Ann and Norman Stanier

Foreword

When you walk through an orchard, it's easy to feel that what you are experiencing is stable – a grouping of trees in particular arrangements. But an orchard is not so much a place as an event, a series of moments becoming and evolving slowly over time. It was this sense of time in the orchard, the slow changes over the course of a year, the openings and releasings, that I wanted to explore in the poems. So the poetry trail is a walk through an orchard undertaken by a particular individual at a specific moment of the year. But the walk is also a way of recovering and discovering: a whole year in one long gulp.

I came to Dragon Orchard for a few days once each month. On these days, chosen mostly at random when I was free, I took my chances with weather and light and atmosphere, and built these moments into the poems. There are naturally poems which tend to reflect a seasonal pattern, and there are poems which record both chance discoveries and significant events, treating the

accidental and the deliberate with equal respect and gravity. My time in the orchard on the days I visited simply consisted of walking and being attentive, of looking and listening and letting my senses and imagination be opened and operated upon by the orchard. You might say that in a sense the orchard walked through me.

I'm very grateful to the Staniers for allowing me to tramp over their ground as and when I liked, and I was grateful for the free hand they gave me. I must also express my thanks to Adrian Johnson of the Arts Council West Midlands, who generously provided the funds to write these poems.

I'm delighted to see these poems in print at last, and I hope your time in the orchard will be as rewarding as mine.

Charles Bennett July 2009.

4 *January*

At dawn the Wassail pig
goes scampering free at last.
She snuffles the ashes of bonfires
and then she turns her attention
to that big white apple in the sky
she's looked at night after night.

We lie in bed and listen
as she goes from tree to tree
saying what she always says:
Hatsful, capsful, three-bushel-bags full,
some left over for the boys to steal
and little heaps under the stairs.

1 *February*

Pruning the trees in winter
is a promise of more we make
by leaving less. It's learning
to see what must go
for the sake of letting in light.

On a deep cold night last week
a fox took the goose away.
As if to show there has to be
a loss before a gain.
As if in his own way
he was letting in the light.

5 *March*

Up by these hawthorn hedges
at the orchard's quiet end
where no one thinks to look,
primroses hidden in the undergrowth
show themselves at last.

Pale yellow flowers of beginning
folded away like a secret
given to the orchard for safe keeping.
New each year and old
as the blackbird's evensong.

2

April

April speaks in blossom:
thousands of flower-mouths open
and the orchard finds its voice
as tongue-buds of dusky red
come blushing out and spill
in a fall of April snow
that will not melt until
the cuckoo is only an echo
and all these visiting bees
have left the orchard speechless.

8 *May*

I found a dead mole one morning
a wet velvet mitten
under the oak tree here.
He must have come up for air
and lay with his mouth wide open
as if about to speak.

After a life underground
with a sky full of roots for company
he must have thought the blossoming trees
angels in the orchard of heaven;
and seeing his work was done,
decided to call it a day.

6 *June*

If you put this apple to your ear
you might just hear the thrushes
who come from miles around
on Midsummer's Eve.

Each has a tree he sits in
and once the orchard's full
they wait till dawn then
all of them sing at once.

Nobody knows what it means,
except perhaps they sense
after their song the darkness
falls a little sooner every day.

July

He promised to meet her here.
Promised they'd marry next morning.
But his father caught him on the doorstep,
locked him in the cellar all night –
she was never the same after that.

They'd find her clutching a suitcase
deep in the middle of winter,
snow coming down like a veil.
Still she returns now and then
keeping her promise to meet him
under their tree at midnight.

11

August

Who looked through this window
When glass was in the frame?
What happened to the pipe from the stove
Which went through that hole in the roof?
When they took off the door
Was it August with thunder in the air?
Who does it open for now?
Whose boots were the last to cross the
Wooden plank laid down across the ditch?
Where's the tree the roof beam
Was growing inside of once?

7 *September*

Four sisters came to pick blackberries
late one September after school.
You could still see spring in their faces
even though winter lay ahead.

And the youngest, the rash one, said:
"Let's never be married, let's stay
the four of us close together".
So they each made a crown of mistletoe
closed their eyes, held hands, and wished…

And the witch of September who was passing
just then in the shape of a crow
granted their wish and turned them
into these four trees;
each of them still holding mistletoe,
blackberries tumbled at their feet.

10

October

The apples have waited all summer
and now the swallows are gone
we hear them start to fall
as if they were trying to tell us:
"It's time we were on our way."

No one is sure how many left last night.
No one is certain how they decide
the moment is ripe. They drop
like eggs which do not break,
which hold inside the seed
of knowing when.

9 *November*

November sleeps in this shed
till the calendar calls his name,
and then he sighs and all at once
the orchard is full of mist.
He touches the pond with frost
and warms himself at night
on embers of apples that burn
beneath the trees. He waits until
he hears December coming up the lane,
then goes to sleep again
and dreams of snow.

12

December

First the Christmas apple
goes round from eldest to youngest
and out beyond them to the blossom
we have not seen. And then
it returns and is given to those
who planted the orchard for us
and further still, from hand to hand,
until it arrives at Adam –
he holds it out for Eve
who hangs it back on the tree,
and all of us grow more innocent
year on year.

The Squire, the Grower

My Great Grandfather, Harry Taylor was the Overseer to Squire Riley who owned the Putley Court Estate. Such are the roots of a succession of events that have led to the production of this slim volume, which even now rests in your hands, or perhaps is being read aloud to you. Subsequent fruitful endeavours tell the story of how John Riley's inspired agronomy of almost 150 years ago brought Harry Taylor's descendants and a peripatetic poet to a fortuitous meeting in the comforting curve of a straw bale wall.

Herefordshire has a long and distinguished tradition of agriculture with worldwide prominence being achieved by its eponymous breed of cattle, Redstreak cider apples, unique perry pears and distinctive hop yards. However, agriculture is by its very nature always evolving and just as now, soft fruit and mini hops are being increasingly

grown, so in the late 19th century John Riley realised that he needed to increase the productivity of his estate. He graduated from Trinity College Cambridge in 1870, became a leading agronomist, travelled the world and as befitted a member of the Woolhope Club and the Royal Horticultural Society, carefully researched his options. He decided to replace his mixed farms with more intensive orcharding and took a risk by appointing the young, and by all accounts, somewhat loquacious Harry Taylor as his Orchard Manager. These two between them transformed the physical landscape of Putley, as well as subtly altering the social fabric of the village in ways that continue to the present day. Harry and his wife Amelia lived at Fosbury and produced eight children, among them my grandfather and namesake, Norman. The Taylors were incomers from over Droitwich way, bringing with them experience, energy and new blood. Norman married Dorothy Kate Brookes, daughter of the last miller, whose family had been in the parish for centuries. A look at the gravestones in Putley churchyard will reveal their procreativity and the number of houses with

which they have been associated. When the Putley Court Estate was sold in the early 1920s the ambitious Norman Taylor bought a twenty-two acre block of orchards. He and Dorothy built a new house and my mother Babs and her sister Monica walked up the road from Glebe Farm, Aylton to take up residence at Orchard Croft, Putley. Apart from the war, Babs then lived there until she was lovingly carried out in a wicker coffin some 80 years later.

During the Second World War Babs nursed in India, while Monica drove fire engines and kept up local morale. Norman was ill and died in 1945, so Dorothy ran the farm with the help of local labourers and during that time the orchard provided work and a living wage for the family and a number of other workers. When Babs returned from India she married Ken Stanier, son of the local Station Master and he moved into Orchard Croft to join her, her mother Dorothy and Grandmother Kate. It was into this lively extended fruit growing family that I was born in December 1947, followed by my brother Clive the next autumn. Our early days were spent closely allied to the soil. We had our own well for water, a generator for electricity and grew almost all our own food. Ken and Babs ventured into pigs, chickens, turkeys, ran a milk round and even an apple processing plant to supplement the seasonal income from the fruit. Clive and I stone picked, fruit picked, tree climbed, hauled countless trailer loads of fruit to Ashperton Station and loaded goods wagons for national distribution. We stacked lorries bound for

Birmingham and Bolton, we mowed and sprayed, hedged, planted and peeled. The family undertook almost all the orchard work with help from a few seasonal pickers but still further income was needed from other sources and Ken became a Youth Leader in Ledbury.

we mowed, sprayed, hedged, planted and peeled.

During secondary school I became interested in outdoor activities and, after training in Exeter as a PE Teacher, did Voluntary Service Overseas in Jamaica and eventually became an Outward Bound Instructor. Ann and I met on the edge of Dartmoor at the Devon Outward Bound School. I completed a Masters' degree in Washington State in the USA and we married in 1977 before working and travelling around the world. I then ran a series of urban outdoor activity projects but we always hoped to one day return to Herefordshire. We came back to Putley in 1993 where we built our own eco-friendly house in the orchard, moving into Dragon House in 1995, some 70 years after Norman and Dorothy had built Orchard Croft on the other side of the plantation. Our plan had been to work alongside Babs and Ken to learn our trade and gradually take on the running of the farm. However, Ken died just two months after our return. This steepened our learning curve just a little, but Babs had had a lifetime's experience on which we could draw and we forged a wonderful working relationship which continued until she was well into her 80s.

Now, some fifteen years since our homecoming, the farm has continued to change and evolve reflecting the lifestyle and demand of consumers and the challenges of sustaining a small orchard. Not long after our return it became increasingly difficult to sell our fruit. The local wholesale market in Hereford was taken over, not once but twice, and changed its buying policy. The small scale outlets which took the poorer quality fruit, disappeared. Supermarkets increasingly held sway and prices were very much held down. We began to realise that our assets were the environment and surroundings as well as the actual orchard produce, and we needed to find new and innovative ways to add value to our enterprise. Thus, in October 2001, we launched Dragon Orchard Cropsharers, which gives its members the opportunity to reconnect with the countryside through a quarterly series of weekends, newsletters and a share of the crop at harvest time. This unique Community Supported Agriculture scheme has grown to over 100 members and is now one of the key drivers of our business. Following the success of Cropsharers we decided to plant a new orchard with different types of fruit trees including 20 varieties of apples, aptly named Dorothy's Orchard. These trees are available for sponsorship through our Sponsor A Tree scheme which further enhances our orchard community.

May you enjoy it as we have and may you also, just ever so slightly, fall under the spell of the Shire.

For several years we have had some of our fruit made into juice and cider by other local producers. In 2007 we met Simon and Hannah Day who had recently moved into the village. Simon is a wine maker of some repute who had produced cider while working in Jersey and together we set up our own cider and apple juice company, Once Upon A Tree that was launched in May 2008. Since its inception it has produced an innovative and award-winning range of juice and cider that utilises our fruitful resources.

Whilst furthering our involvement in our local community, we hosted a Ledbury Poetry Festival workshop in 2003 and the then Festival Director, Charles Bennett, became embroiled in our orchard and in our lives. Charles was greatly inspired by spending time in the orchard and he suggested taking a year and visiting once a month to capture 'that' moment. Our patch of land and his imagination has given rise to this slender tome you have before you. The paths of the Squire, the Growers and the Poet have become inextricably linked and you now have become a part of the story. May you enjoy it as we have and may you also, just ever so slightly, fall under the spell of the Shire.

Photo: Courtesy of LEAF

Photo: Simon Day

The publishers would like to
acknowledge the generosity of:

The Big Apple Association

The Pennington-Mellor-Munthe Charity Trust

Mrs Geraldine Ablett

Julie and Richard Crompton

Dragon Orchard

Putley, Ledbury, Herefordshire, HR8 2RG

www.dragonorchard.co.uk

FORDSON